Whales, Dolphins & Sharks

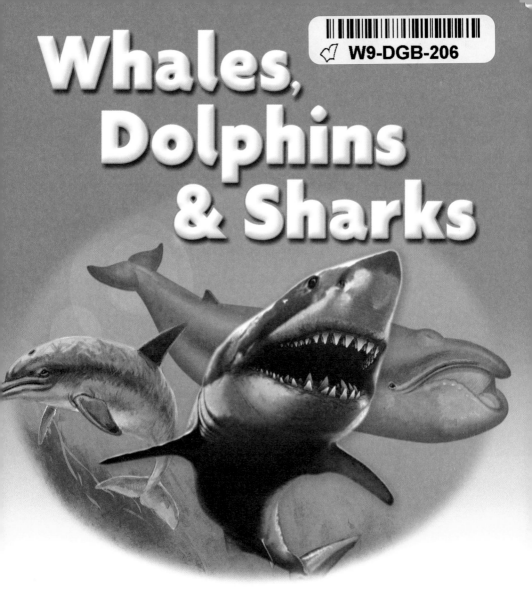

LEVEL 2 READER

Humbback Whale

Whales are the largest animals on Earth. They are mammals that live in the sea. Like all mammals, they breathe air. They exhale, or "blow," out of a blowhole on top of the head.

The humpback whale is about 50 feet long. It weighs more than 20 tons—as much as four big elephants!

Humpback whales make noises that sound like singing. Each male whale sings his own song.

Baby whales feed on milk from their mothers. When the calves are larger, they will eat fish and krill. Krill are small shrimp-like animals.

Gray Whale

Look at this gray whale and her calf.
Do you see all the spots? Some of those are
barnacles. Barnacles are small animals with
shells that attach to objects in the sea, like
rocks, boats—and whales!

The gray whale can do tricks! It can jump
high out of the water, "ride" waves, roll onto
its side, and "wave" its fin.

Bowhead Whale

This big, playful whale is a bowhead whale. It has smooth skin that helps it glide through the water. This whale does not have teeth. It has *baleen* (bay-leen). Baleen is made of stiff hair-like strips.

When the whale closes its mouth, the water pushes out through the baleen. The fish and krill stay in the mouth.

Right Whale

The right whale is a giant of the sea. Long ago, sailors thought these whales were the "right" ones to catch. New laws have saved many right whales from hunters.

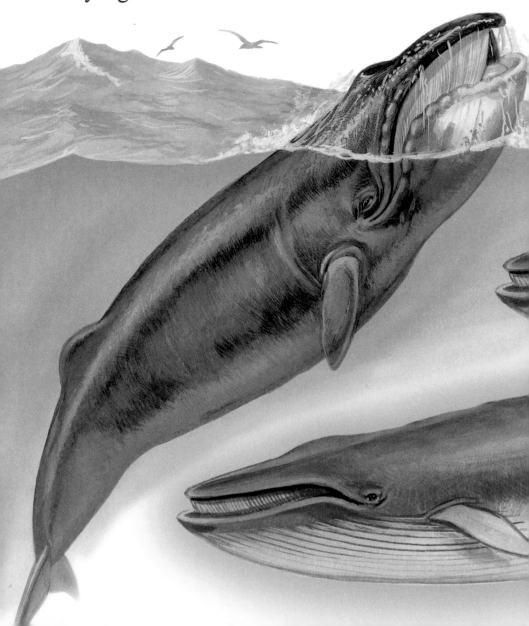

Sei Whale

The sei whale lives in the cold waters of the Arctic and Antarctica. In winter, sei whales swim to warmer waters, where females give birth to calves.

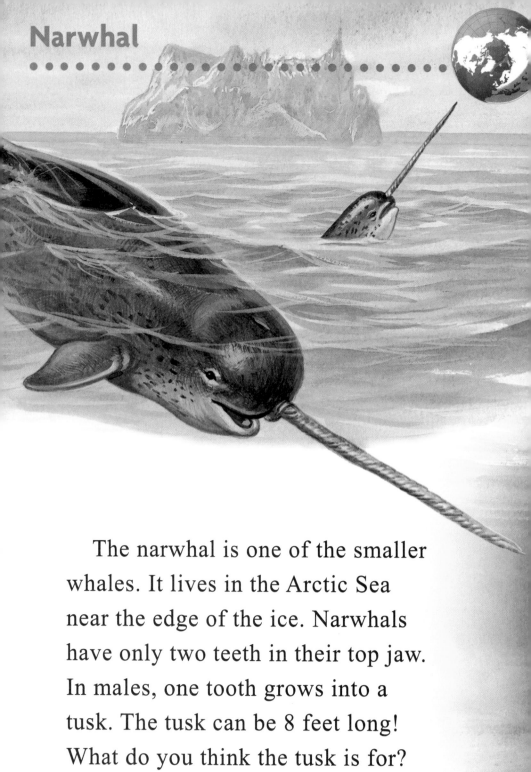

The narwhal is one of the smaller whales. It lives in the Arctic Sea near the edge of the ice. Narwhals have only two teeth in their top jaw. In males, one tooth grows into a tusk. The tusk can be 8 feet long! What do you think the tusk is for?

Beluga Whale

The beluga whale also lives in the Arctic Sea. It has thick fat, called blubber, to keep it warm.

A beluga's skin is white. This makes it hard to see a beluga around the ice. The beluga makes interesting sounds: chirps, whistles, squawks, and clicks.

Orca

The orca is sometimes called a killer whale. It is not really a whale. It is a very large dolphin. Like other dolphins, the orca has teeth. Orcas are smart hunters. They live in groups, called pods, with six to thirty other orcas.

Risso's Dolphin

This animal looks like a small whale, but it is a dolphin. Its skin is covered with white scars. They get these scars from battles with other dolphins, and also from squid—their favorite food.

Risso's dolphins like to swim in deep, warm waters and hunt in groups, side by side.

Dolphin

Dolphins are lively animals. They often leap out of the water. They also like to ride the waves in front of ships.

Dolphins live in pods. They hunt for schools of fish or even squid and octopuses.

Dolphins are smart and curious. Sometimes they swim up to scuba divers and travel alongside them.

Striped Dolphin

The striped dolphin has dark
lines on its sides. These dolphins are good
acrobats. They can jump high above the water
and do amazing flips!

Like other dolphins, they sleep while
swimming slowly on the top of the water.
They keep their heads
out of the water
to breathe. Their
tails move even
when they're
asleep!

Common Dolphin

The common dolphin is a fast swimmer. These dolphins like warm ocean waters, but they sometimes swim into rivers.

In spring, the females give birth to calves. When a calf is tired, the mother lifts it onto her back and swims along the top of the water.

Blind River Dolphin

The blind river dolphin has tiny eyes. It uses other senses to find its way through the muddy river water. Long ago, many of these dolphins lived in the big rivers of India. But none have been seen for a long time.

Amazon River dolphins live in the rivers of South America. Their skin color can be dark gray, light gray, or even pink! It's very hard to catch one of these dolphins with a net. The dolphin senses the trap and jumps over it.

Whitetip Reef Shark

Sharks are not mammals. Sharks are fish. They do not need to come to the top of the water to breathe air.

Do you see the small white tip on this shark's back-fin? That gives this shark its name—whitetip reef shark.

The great white shark is very big!
It can grow to more than 30 feet long!

This shark hunts for fish, seals, and
turtles. There are rows and rows of
sharp teeth in its huge mouth. It likes
to hunt in deep waters, but sometimes
it comes close to shore.

Baby tiger sharks have stripes that look like tiger stripes. As the sharks get older, they lose these stripes.

Tiger sharks—like all sharks—have no bones. They only have firm tissue called *cartilage* (like the cartilage of your ears).

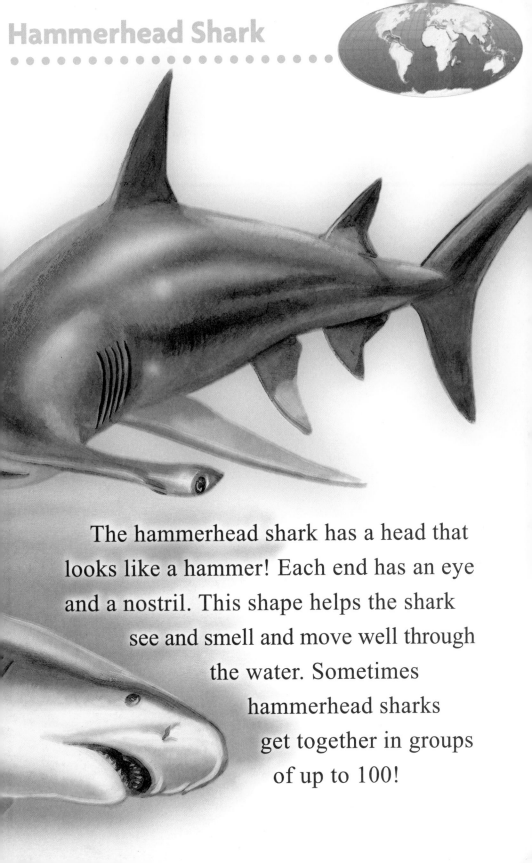

Hammerhead Shark

The hammerhead shark has a head that looks like a hammer! Each end has an eye and a nostril. This shape helps the shark see and smell and move well through the water. Sometimes hammerhead sharks get together in groups of up to 100!

Stingray

Stingrays are related to sharks. Like sharks, they have no bones. They are flat fish with wide fins. They flap their fins to move through the water. Stingrays can grow up to 6½ feet long.

The stingray has a sharp barb on the end of its tail. It has poison in this barb. When the stingray strikes with its tail, it stings!

Manta Ray

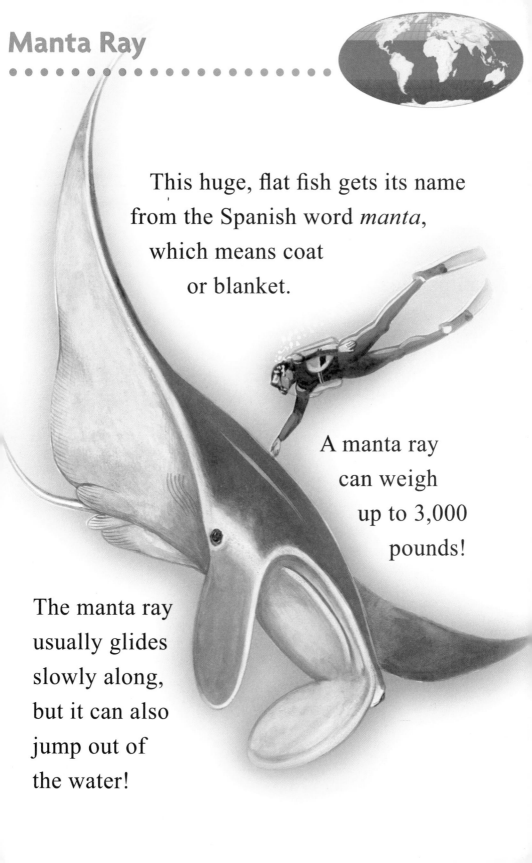

This huge, flat fish gets its name from the Spanish word *manta*, which means coat or blanket.

A manta ray can weigh up to 3,000 pounds!

The manta ray usually glides slowly along, but it can also jump out of the water!

Whale Shark

This big animal can live 100 to 150 years! It is not a whale. It is a shark— a whale shark. It is the biggest fish in the world. It swims through the water and gulps food into its large mouth.

Whales, dolphins, and sharks sure are amazing!